Sometimes You Need To

Kick Your Own Butt

Strategies for Success by

PEGINE ECHEVARRIA

Contact Team Pegine at www.pegine.com, 904/280-8806 or email info@pegine.com for information on purchasing additional copies of this publication, or to book Pegine for your next event.

Acknowledgments

Often in my life, I have found myself having to push myself to take actions that I haven't wanted to take, even though I knew they were good for me.

The easier softer, way usually looked more attractive, though. Sometimes I took the easier way only to find that it didn't lead me to the dreams and goals I had for myself, and that it carried consequences that weren't so easy to deal with after all.

Over time I learned what it would take for me to kick myself in the butt, push myself forward one step at a time, and, as a result of the pushing, prodding and kicking I gave myself, get the rewards I was after.

I was not alone, though. There were people alongside that were my cheerleaders, tour guides and at times worked the pulleys. This is my thanks to them.

My first words of thanks go to God. I know there have been times that I've yelled at You, times that I've laughed at Your jokes, and times that I've been grateful for the many

www.pegine.com

lessons, gifts and insights You've given me. Thank You for always being there for me.

Without my soul mate and my dearest friend, my successes in the world of business would be meaningless. David gives my life meaning. He teases, annoys me, loves me and cheers me on. He is my critic, devil's advocate and greatest promoter. By the way, you can always call him when you want me. Thank you, David.

My son Kenneth taught me that strength and going after your dreams can be done quietly. That determination can be done quietly beneath the surface. He is a soldier in the Army National Guard, quietly pursuing his dream of being an officer. He is already a gentleman and what's more, he is one of the most loyal, gentle, funny, strong leaders I've encountered. Thank you for giving me solace when times got rough, Kenneth.

My daughter Andrea taught me that it is what you do on a daily basis, no matter what, that moves you towards your dreams. She is an accomplished, funny and hard-working determined young lady. Her boot is made of pure steel; it's a joy to watch her push herself to higher and higher levels. Thank you, Andrea, for teaching me about persistence.

Then there's the woman who applauds me continually. She has listened to years and years of stories, defeats, wins, and dreams. She read and edited my work for decades, and she believed in me when I didn't believe in myself. Through shear determination she gave me a life that was rich, different and full. Thank you, Mom.

If it weren't for Joe Tee this book would not be here. For the last nine years Joe has masterfully molded me into an author. His insights, editing, careful questioning and unwavering faith in my abilities has enabled me to create products that inspire others to take action. He is spiritually connected to a source of great insight and shares it willingly. Thank you, Joe.

My thanks go also to Matthew Richards of Digital Alchemy of Sarasota (www.dasrq.com), the incredibly talented graphic designer who was able to bring the cover of this book to life.

The following friends and mentors also deserve a round of applause: Craig Austad, Denise Balthis, Paula Roderick, Cindy Bethel, Jacksonville Women's Business Center, Jacksonville Chamber of Commerce, Bob Baldwin, Sandy Bartow, Greg DeVino, CPA from Ennis, Pellum & Associates, CPAs, and Celeste Turain from Wachovia Bank. Thank you all so much.

Finally, I wanted to thank you, the reader, for investing your precious time and energy in reviewing what follows. But I didn't have your email address. So drop me a line, and maybe I can thank you in the next book!

Pegine
pegine@pegine.com

Table of Contents

www.pegine.com
©2002, 2005, 2007 Pegine Echevarria

First Things First

It's time to kick butt ... and take responsibility for changing your own world for the better! Each chapter features four easy to read segments designed to help you do just that.

Quotes – Sayings that inspire and tell it like it is

Try its – Incremental, step by step techniques that take you a little further to a being the person you were meant to be. They worked for me, and they'll work for you!

Kick Butt Actions –State-changing, world-changing strategies that *immediately* propel you to a new level. They take courage. **I learned a long time ago that courage = fear plus action.** So ... feel the fear and kick butt anyway!

Stories – Accounts that enthuse, motivate, and kick your own butt. Read them and *take action*! Let's get started!

Quote

"We are responsible for the daily actions
we do or don't undertake to move towards
our dream.
We are NOT responsible for the
outcome...the outcome comes from a higher
source.
Do not confuse your own lack of action with
a message from a higher source.
Your action -- or lack of action --- is your
only responsibility."

-- Pegine *Echevarria~*

Try Its

1. List as many words as you can that
   describe the person you want to be.
   For example; powerful, dynamic,
   positive, lovable, capable,
   philanthropic, stable, financially
   wealthy.

2. Just for today, think how a person
   with those characteristics would act if
   they were living your life.

3. Just as an experiment … act that way
   and see what happens.

www.pegine.com
©2002, 2005, 2007 Pegine Echevarria

Take time this month to review where you've been. Keep a written log.

So often we think we haven't done anything, or accomplished anything … until we review all that we have done. This log is not only for work but also a review of your relationships, your physical health, and your attitude.

Once you review it congratulate yourself on your actions and successes. Start right now to log your actions for this year. Next year at this time you will see all that you have to celebrate!

Use a table to log calls, sales and actions. Use a journal to share your emotional and spiritual growth. I strongly suggest keeping a "gratitude book" to keep you focused on blessings.

www.pegine.com
©2002, 2005, 2007 Pegine Echevarria

Dreams Do Come True

Dreams have a way of including challenges. That is good because it is only through overcoming the challenges that our dreams are turned into reality and appreciated.

Over the last few years my family and I made some major positive changes. With those changes, however, came many challenges. Meeting the challenges daily became a great way to discover how positive, daily habits could make unusual stressful times easier to deal with.

Let me give you the low-down. We moved from the Northeast to the Southeast and transferred two children in middle school to a new school. My husband changed his career of 20 years to a brand new, totally different career (and, in the process, had to go from suit and tie to shorts). He sold his business and is learning a brand new craft.

That's not all. My dog contracted a rare disease, and we ended up homeless for three weeks, because of delays out of our control. Finally, we all had to tearfully say good-bye to dear friends and business associates that we came to cherish. Amazingly, though, I have never felt more alive, courageous and liberated in my life!

Why? Because our family made a choice to look at change as *opportunity in the now*. Now, right now, is an opportunity for everyone to truly create, imagine and develop a life that is filled with every joy that you can imagine! This is renewal! It is a time for birth, a time for new energy and new opportunities. It's a time for dreaming.

Here are some strategies you can use to handle dreams and their challenges – to give birth to your *opportunity in the now*.

Dream Book

Distractions can take us away from our

dreams and purpose. Life often seems to pull the rug from us. We can get caught up in the daily duties of living that we often forget to focus on what we want and who we want to be.

I have used dream books for years to stay on a steady course. It reminds me of what and who I want to be. The dream book helps me visualize exactly what I want to experience in my life.

The dream book is a photo album filled with words and pictures that describe your ideal life. On the first page, use words to describe the person you would like to be; honest, energetic, happy, sociable, loving, smart, supportive, and rich. Make it a long list. Think of the way you want your family, friends, business associates, and community members to describe you.

On the next few pages, cut out from magazines the words and any headlines that describe the kind of work you want to do and how much you want to earn. Create a statement of how you want to be in that job. How successful do you want to be? How are you going to measure that success?

Make sure that your dream book covers the five areas of your life: physical, emotional, spiritual, intellectual, and fiscal. Every morning, read and look over your dream book. Some days you will read it quickly, other days you will spend a lot of time looking over each page.

The book keeps you focused and makes you believe that dreams can come true.

The dream book is for your eyes only. Don't share it with others. People will want to protect you by telling you not to dream, because you may get hurt.

Trust me; *you will get hurt more deeply by not dreaming.*

Start your dream book today! Let me know how you are doing by visiting me at Pegine.com and dropping a line. If your experience is anything like mine, you will be amazed over time at how many dreams have come true and how you have become more focused and energetic about your dreams.

Journal

We often think and think and think and think … without really focusing on *what* we are choosing to run through our minds, and *how*. Sometimes negative thought patterns go on and on and we never stop to say, "whoa, what am I thinking?"

A journal enables you to write your thoughts on paper and give yourself the positive reinforcement we all need to get us through life with a smile.

Each day, take some time try to write down your thoughts -- the good, the bad, and the ugly. Cry as you write, get angry as you write, celebrate as you write, just get your thoughts down on paper.

End each journal writing with five specific things that you are grateful for.

Think of all the possible candidates: Shelter from the rain, oxygen, good food to eat, fingers for scratching your head, a bed to sleep in, a computer that enables you to write, or kissing your child's head.

As you continue doing this on a daily basis, you will find yourself improving in your ability to change your negative thoughts into more positive thoughts.
Go for it, journal writing works!

Sing Your Song

When you are in the shower, in your car, or walking by yourself, make up a song about how special you are and all of your qualities. I start out with the melody of Yankee Doodle

Dandy or something else corny. I add words that celebrate who I am.

Okay, it sounds wacky, but it works.

It fills me up with such happiness about life that I want to shout it out to the world. My kids sing their own songs about themselves. People who sing their own songs, I find, are happier and more content with themselves than people who do not.

Daily Actions Reap Rewards.

All these activities are daily investments in you. Your self-esteem and positive outlook are created and owned by you. Your parents, husband, lovers, friends or coaches can not make you feel good or bad about yourself. *You* are the only one with that power, because it is your perceptions of who you are that decide how you feel about yourself. The three steps outlined above will guide you to filling yourself up with positive self-love. Love yourself ----- you're worth it!

Quote

"It takes more than love to create a supportive, loving relationship. It takes self-improvement, humor, thick skin, honest communication and knowing that you must go within to find your true love."

--Pegine Echevarria ~

When you are feeling stressed - take a time out.

Go sit in a quiet chair or if you are in desperate times go to the bathroom and lock the door.

Put your hand on your heart and concentrate on the beating of your heart.

When you feel the rhythm of your heart quietly say to yourself (following the beat) "All is well, I am loved. All is well, I'm alive."

You will be calmed and centered.

Kick Butt
Actions

Here are three more actions that you can take on a daily basis that will support your dreams, renew your spirit and calm your soul.

1 - Every morning, take half an hour for yourself. Be up before everyone else or take time during the early mid morning. During that half hour, go through this life saving ritual:

- Write in your "moan-groan-gee-I-learned-something-about-myself" journal. Mine is not a fancy book. It's a beat up composition book. Use it to write about the disagreement you had with your spouse, your fears about your business, or your challenges with your children – or anything else worth learning from.

- Read two motivational daily meditation books. Make sure they have plenty of uplifting quotes and insights (like this one does).

- Ask your Higher Power/God/ The Universe to guide you in the day to show you where you can serve others and how you can improve yourself and stay "on purpose" in the business of turning your dream into reality.

2 - During the day, speak to a minimum of two people who support, love and want you to succeed. For me, one is always my husband and the other is my buddy.   My friend and I made an agreement to kick each other in the butt and keep us focused on our

personal growth and the growth of our business. Share your plans and commit to making them happen. It's great, it's a pain and it works.

3 - Plan your work and work your plan during the day. When you hit challenges, which you will, take a moment to remind yourself that you are not built to do everything. You are human and striving. (Hint: Closing your eyes and touching your heart keeps you close to yourself.)

www.pegine.com

Overcoming the "IT" Bug

Talking about IT, planning IT, and thinking about IT, don't add up to the one action that makes the most difference in our lives --- doing IT. Whatever IT is.

IT can be writing a letter to the friends you miss. IT can be going to the gym three times a week. IT can be smiling and saying something nice to each member of your family, or IT can be making that tenth cold call for your business.

For such a small word, IT can become extremely powerful, becoming bigger and bigger in our minds, as we avoid taking the necessary action that would remove IT from our line of vision.

IT often has several effects on our mental and emotional state. We have a tendency to beat ourselves up, because we haven't dealt with a particular issue, however we define IT. That ever present four letter world "fear" holds us back from dealing with actions that would make our lives a whole lot easier.

IT can make us run for cover - literally hiding under our quilts for comfort. Yet, even as we seek refuge, IT seems to loom over us and send us into an angry frenzy, making us yell, blame, act out, cover up and drive ourselves nuts, as we procrastinate further from doing IT.

How do we tame this small, aggressive, bug called IT? Here are some strategies that actually work.

- Have a goal buddy. This can be a friend, classmate, business associate, husband or wife. It can be different people for different IT bugs. Make yourself accountable. "I will call you up this afternoon at two, to tell you that I have dealt with IT." Be clear with your buddy. If you don't complete the task and call them, make sure that they will call you and remind you of your contract.

- Decide that today you will spend 15 minutes dealing with IT. The art of getting started can begin by telling yourself you will only spend a short time on IT. Set a timer to confirm that you can stop after 15 minutes. Once we begin and are involved with IT we will stay with IT until the job is done.

- Break IT into smaller tasks. IT may be just too big to handle all at once. Breaking the outcome into smaller and smaller defined tasks enables you to deal with little tiny bits and pieces. Decide you will take a step at a time. Just moving towards IT will make a difference.

- Don't get caught up with quality, quantity or perfectionism. Whatever IT is, just decide you will do *something* towards completion – and no, this does not always need to be your best work. Taking the action is the key to removing the power IT has over us. Once we begin to take the action we can then decide the quality of our actions.

We all have an IT. Removal of IT begins with just a small action - much smaller than this tiny word - it. Remember, IT begins with **I**.

"You have a choice. Either you become a legacy by sharing your wisdom learned through experiences ... or you fade away, never to be remembered, because you refuse to share that wisdom."

~Pegine Echevarria

Try Its

- Look around you.

- Identify at least one person of a different ethnic and/or economic background who has the potential of becoming great in his or her career.

- Write down two things that you can share with that person that would guide him or her to reaching their potential. Feeling really brave? Share those ideas

- Identify another person who has the qualities that you would like to achieve.

- Write down one a question that you would pose to that person.

- When given the opportunity ask, do so and then LISTEN.

www.pegine.com

Kick Butt
Actions

To find a mentor for yourself:

- Define what you need help with.

- Join professional associations and networking groups to meet and identify potential mentors.

- Get involved. Talk to a variety of people.

- Identify who has what you want or need.

- Get to them. Offer to help them with a project (volunteer for them).

- ASK FOR HELP.

- Then listen, and use or discard the advice.

www.pegine.com
©2002, 2005, 2007 Pegine Echevarria

- SHARE information about your decisions and outcomes with the person who helped you. (There is nothing more frustrating for mentors than not knowing whether or not you were successful after they helped you.)

To be a mentor:

- Listen.

- Ask questions.

- Share your own Experience, Strength and Hope about how you cope in similar situations.

- Don't expect to hear about the outcomes.

Seek Positive Opportunities
Where You Are Now

Bees look for pollen to make honey wherever they are. I've seen bees buzz in junkyards and in beautiful gardens. They find sweetness next to the concrete of the city as well as in the pastures of the country. It doesn't matter where they are; they seek the opportunities for sweetness. They are our teachers.

How often during your day do you seek the sweetness? Did you take the chance to make a new friend, initiate a business relationship, or say or do something positive for a child? How often do we miss the opportunity of a lifetime, because we are busy convincing ourselves that there is no opportunity to be had?

Taking the time to see opportunities and miracles *where we are* requires us to stop and take into account the specifics this very moment – where we are, what we are thinking, what we are feeling. Rushing around during the day we rarely stop and take an account of where we are, and who we are choosing to be that very moment.

Take the time *today* to focus on what kind of person you want to be. How do you want to be perceived in the world? What actions are you taking to be that person? Do you want to be perceived as being powerful, kind, generous, sociable, intelligent, articulate, compassionate, strong, decisive and caring?

Next, observe yourself during the day. Are you acting the way you want to be perceived? If not -- change your actions. Acting as though you already are the way you want to be perceived is the secret to becoming that person.

Observe the people, objects and things around you. Begin by focusing on the flower outside your window or on your way to work. Truly observe it. The texture, the colors, the way the light hits it and how it feels in your hand.

Focus on the miracle in your sight and in your hand. Look out in your world and focus on the people in the elevator, smile and appreciate them. Focus on your co-workers positive attributes while continuing to focus on your own behavior and your own 'being'.

Jot down the opportunities that are being placed in your path. Observe them and act on them. Don't discount them or let fear stop you from taking action. They are being placed in your path for your positive outcomes.

Positive opportunities can be presented in the form of connections between people, jobs, money, teachings, messages, gifts and an endless array of signals, warnings, and signs. The key is being open to them. Start by observing, then receive and accept the gifts. You deserve them.

Quote

"Every moment is an opportunity to choose your attitude. It really is your choice how you act and more importantly how you RE-act. Choose wisely – your quality of life depends on it."

~Pegine Echevarria, MSW~

Try Its

Here are three magic ways to change your attitude quickly so you can find opportunities in what is happening right now:

1. If you are furious at someone, STOP TALKING. Walk away. Count to ten. Let go.

> Now, go to another room, take a pillow and pound it a minimum of 30 times. Or go to your car, roll up your windows and scream at the top of your lungs – let every inch of your body express your anger and frustration by taking action in private.

> Alternatively, go to a private place and write out your fury on paper -- not in an e-mail message or any other medium than good old-fashioned paper. Use every name in the book if necessary. Write the anger, express it,

until it is expended, *then rip up or burn what you have written*. Then figure out, calmly, what needs to happen next in the real world.

2. Play the game of 'what if.'

Sometimes we don't know a different way of reacting when a situation arises. Maybe we always break into tears when we are teased, or we have a habit of getting angry and taking things personally.

Practice conscious "Re-actions" *before* the next stressful situation occurs. Think of "what if" scenarios. When I'm teased 'what if' I reacted by laughing? 'What if' I had the confidence to confront the teaser what would that look like? Think about the different reactions you could potentially have. Next time you actually find yourself in these situations you can choose to use the new reaction and see what happens. Life is a game, so make it interesting.

3. Notice the physical manifestations of your attitude.

Instead of automatically naming it – let's say "scared" -- look for other emotions or attitudes that have similar physical manifestations. "Scared" and "excited" manifest themselves in very similar ways. Choose excited over scared. Try using the word that supports you; see which leaves you better equipped to find opportunities in the present reality.

www.pegine.com
©2002, 2005, 2007 Pegine Echevarria

Kick Butt
Actions

Our attitudes EITHER hold us back or propel us forward. Which is it? "Kick your own butt" by taking personal responsibility for answering that question.

Is your attitude one of self-defeat, victim mentality or minority hopelessness? Or are you living a new and different attitude of winning, of power-survivor, of victory? Are you looking at yourself as the persecuted minority, or as the powerful new majority?

We all have a story. How we view our story can change our whole perception of our life and ourselves.

For years I lived the "Poor me – my dad abandoned me when I was young" story. Until one day I stopped and asked myself -- "What my life would be like if he was

www.pegine.com
©2002, 2005, 2007 Pegine Echevarria

around? Would I be who I am today?" And then came the realization: "I love who I am ... without my story I wouldn't be me!"

1. Write your 'story' -- the one that makes you angry, depressed, or frustrated. The one that says "if only..." The one that you've nurtured and used as an excuse not to take action and look for opportunity in the present situation. Maybe you don't have a college degree, aren't rich, aren't tall and aren't thin. What is YOUR excuse story? Write it down.

2. Or talk the story into a tape recorder.

3. Now read it over (or listen to it) and identify the "victim" or "poor me language." Then change it to victor-winner language.

4. Make the story about how you overcame the odds to succeed in

reaching this moment, instead of how something held you back.

The point is to REWRITE the story so it's about your survival and your willingness to embrace what's happening RIGHT NOW. Then repeat it to yourself each and every day.

Chocolate or Vanilla?

Therapist to woman: "How do you feel about being in assertiveness counseling?"

Woman: "I'm not sure -- I haven't asked my husband yet."

"I don't know. It doesn't matter." Is your internal power being drained away because you give your power of choice away? Every time we don't choose our reality, or allow someone else to choose for us, we give a little of our power away. If it really doesn't matter to us, then why not choose something – anything – just for the exercise that will develop our choosing muscle?

The act of choice gives us responsibility, which in turn leads to respect and self-respect. Responsibility means the ability to respond. Not choosing is negating our ability to respond.

When we don't act responsibly, or use our ability to respond/choose, we send messages to ourselves and others that we are not confident in our ability to choose wisely and that we believe others are smarter, wiser and better that us. Every time someone mispronounces our name and we say, "It's okay", we are saying that the name we chose to accept for ourselves is not that important. On the other hand, if we help people learn how important it is to pronounce our name, they will respect us for it. (If you don't like your name - choose another name and legally change it. It is your choice.)

As human beings we have the freedom to choose. Good or evil, sweet or sour, happy or sad, for better or worse, each and every one of us choose how we are treated by others, how our relationships look, how our jobs and careers satisfy us. It becomes a simple choice of chocolate and vanilla.

No one else needs to understand your choices. You need to understand that your choices are

www.pegine.com

just that-- YOUR CHOICES. You have the ability to respond to each and every situation *by choosing*. If you don't like how things are going - choose differently. If you aren't happy in your present situation, either choose to be happy, change your approach to the situation, look for alternative solutions, or *get out of the situation*. It is your choice.

Choice is not easy. Choosing from different opportunities can be overwhelming and perplexing. However, not choosing is actually choosing. You're choosing to lose the opportunity to choose. We often do this when we procrastinate and retreat.

"No one can make you feel inferior without your consent." When I first read this quote from Eleanor Roosevelt, I chose to put it on my wall, simply because I didn't understand it and I wanted to study it for a while. Why would I give someone else my consent to make me feel inferior? I often felt inferior -- but "they" made me feel that way, didn't they? As I began to study how we build up

our self-esteem and how responsibility, choice and seeking opportunity are part of our God given rights, I began to understand what Mrs. Roosevelt was getting at.

We can choose to perceive others' behavior in any way we want.

We can see their behavior as loving or destructive. We can see others as funny or annoying. We can choose to be angry or happy. It is our choice.

Choice is both your right and your responsibility. Each time we exercise our ability and right to choose how we want our life to be today, we grow in self-respect. When we use our given power, when we use the talents and blessings we have been given we give the gift of self-love to ourselves. And with self-love we can achieve the greatness that each of us is destined to have.

Choose wisely. This is the only life you have!

*"If you truly want to achieve your dreams
you need to have a dream team that will help
you learn to CHOOSE, rather than accept
choices made on your behalf. A group of
coaches, mentors and buddies should push
you, inspire you, teach you and be honest
with you about when you're not CHOOSING
your reality."*

~Pegine Echevarria, MSW~

Try Its

1. *Attend a new group session of some kind.* Look in your local paper for a group that interests you. Maybe you want to start your own business. Go to the Small Business Administration and join one of their new business groups. Perhaps you're a "stay at home" mom. Choose to get better at something in your life. Find a group that supports your growth -- a reading group, a financial investment club, a moms of toddlers group. Or, even better, you can choose to start your own group.

2. *Create a mastermind group.* If you are in a career or have been in business for awhile, I highly recommend that you create a powerful mastermind group. A mastermind group is a small group of people (typically between four and six) that meets twice a month, once a month or once a quarter. You plan-- set goals and hold each other accountable --while

celebrating the big and small steps you make
to living the life you choose to live.

www.pegine.com
©2002, 2005, 2007 Pegine Echevarria

Kick Butt
Actions

1. Get a coach for your personal and professional success. There are all types of coaches for personal and professional success. Get someone who comes with recommendations, someone you feel comfortable with.

2. Create a Power Team. List up to 25 people – not necessarily family members – who can advise you, send you referrals, give you information, and help you find information that will support you. Keep in contact with them. Mail each person on the list a postcard, call, or send an email at least once a month.

3. Network. If you don't have 10 people to put on your list, get involved in some activities. Join organizations and committee work in your community, work, spiritual center, or school. Start meeting people and create a network for yourself. The more people you

know, the better your odds are of being able
to implement what you choose in life.

Rejection: Part Of Life

We have all faced rejection. Maybe we didn't get into the college we wanted, or the date we hoped to have never materialized, perhaps you made overtures to your husband and he just wasn't interested. How we deal with rejection depends on our maturity and the confidence we have in ourselves.

When we are rejected we can point fingers at others for our sadness, depression, loneliness, and feelings at failure. We can choose to embrace negative feelings, or we can choose a different course.

Others are not responsible for the feelings we have, only we are. Only we can make ourselves feel inferior, and only we can make ourselves feel good about who we are.

One of the ways we make ourselves feel good is to speak intelligently to ourselves about rejection. If we were put off during a cold call, we might personalize the rejection. "Of course they wouldn't want to speak to me; I'm a nobody. I'm just a salesperson." Is that the best lesson to draw from the experience? Is that what it really means?

Say your husband rejects your advances tonight, and then you criticize yourself by saying, "I'm not slim, fit and built -- of course he has no desire for me! Why would he?" Is that the best lesson to draw from the experience? Is that what it really "means"?

Passed over for a raise or promotion? What thoughts immediately ran into your head? Are they self-criticism, or some more supportive interpretation of what just happened?

When you no longer make others responsible for your feelings of being inferior, you can change your outlook on rejection.

For instance, if you are a salesperson making cold calls, you eventually learn that a key

aspect of prospecting has to do with numbers.
The bigger the number of people you call, the
better your odds are of getting your foot in
someone's door. Put thirty beans on one side
of your desk and decide to make the thirty
calls. It isn't important if you get thirty
rejections. You must, however, make the
thirty calls. Why the emphasis on a number? If
you make enough calls, you will connect with
someone who will eventually buy. It is a
numbers game. Accept that, and realize that it
isn't about YOU (personally); *it's about the
number of calls you make*.

Your husband can reject advances, and it has
nothing to do with YOU. It can be caused by a
great game that will be on shortly, a terrific
headache caused by pressure at work,
frustration with your kids or simply-not being
in the mood. (Women can identify with that!)
Guess what -- he has those days too.

Getting out of your head is a skill that
requires constant practice and preparation.
Having a positive journal is important.

www.pegine.com
©2002, 2005, 2007 Pegine Echevarria

Whenever the inferiority talk begins inside your head, start writing down things that you are grateful for. Read what you wrote on other days.

No, this isn't denial. Go ahead. If you want, give yourself two minutes to feel the pain of an experience. Then --- get over it! Rejection is part of life! A life full of rewards, love, success and prosperity is also a life that has learned to deal successfully with rejection! Celebrate your ability to move on.

Quote

"Overcoming rejection is not just for people – it's for whole communities, too. Making our community strong, powerful and heard begins with us. It begins with taking a step and asking ourselves, 'What can I do today to help US move on, to help make a positive difference in my community or my family?'"

~ Pegine Echevarria, MSW~

Try Its

Ask yourself the following questions:
- What is bothering me about my community?
- What changes would I want to see happen?
- Has anyone asked me to get involved?

Consider calling local community groups to see what volunteer opportunities are available. But before you sign up, wait 24 hours to ask yourself the following questions:
- Will I learn new skills that would improve my family, career, or self-image?
- Would joining make it easier for me to learn to *move on* in the face of rejection?
- How much time can I give and when is the best time?

(Everyone can give one hour
per week to at least one cause)
- Does this activity match with
  my mission, purpose and
  beliefs?

If you like the answers to these questions
call and ask for the date of the next
meeting. Commit yourself to attend.
Attend two meetings or lunch dates with
the some of the people you will be
involved with.

- Evaluate how you are
  compatible or not.
- Are these people you want to
  affiliate yourself with?
- If not, find a different group –
  recommitting to serve others
  for yourself and your
  community.

After two months write down how your
involvement has made a difference in your
life, the life of your community and the
life of your family.

Kick Butt Actions

- Take action and help teach your community to *move on* and focus on the positive. (Doing so will make it easier for you yourself to *move on*.)
- Make a decision to reach out to your neighbors.

> Bring a cake or a bottle of wine over to a neighbor's home; just to say "I'm glad you're my neighbor". They will be there for you when you need help.

- Every time you enter an elevator…

> Look at the people who are there and say good morning. You have thirty seconds to make an impression on the person in the elevator --- and you just never know who will be in an elevator with you! So be prepared to be your best.

www.pegine.com
©2002, 2005, 2007 Pegine Echevarria

- When you arrive in your office…
  Stop. Look around.
  Purposefully create community
  by interacting with the people
  in your path. Just a hello or
  smile can make a huge
  difference, and encourage
  someone else to respond
  constructively to rejection.

"It's Not Fair!"

"It's just so unfair!"

That's what my 14-year-old shouts when it's time to do his chores. As he rants about his chores, I'm thinking about my mom.

Several weeks ago she was rushed to the hospital for emergency surgery. Three times over the last few weeks I have found myself repeating the same sentence, "It's not fair". Then come the words that bring me back to reality a leave a strange tingle in my ears and heart: *"Get over it."*

Yes, life can be perceived as being unfair. Sometimes we get wonderful rewards and blessings that amaze us. Other times it can feel like we can't go one more step. When there is devastation we want to ask "Why us? Why now?"

Life really is a roller coaster ride: ecstatic highs and dramatic lows. How we deal with these highs and lows can affect perception of the world and ourselves. Here are my top ten tips for keeping centered and sane during the moments when nothing seems fair.

1. Go within. Put your hand on your heart. Feel the steady beat, breath in and ponder on the magnificence of your machine.

2. Say an affirmation that reinforces how great, special and resourceful you are. (For instance: "I have bounced back from much more serious setbacks than this.")

3. Treat yourself to a pedicure or manicure (or whatever floats your boat).

4. Go take a walk. While you are walking concentrate on how your legs feel, concentrate on deep breathing.

5. Notice how many living creature and animals are around you. Concentrate on their life: how they move, look and survive.

6. Tell people around you how important they are to you.

7. Make sure you are eating well. Eat lots of fruits and vegetables during stressful times.

8. Sing a really silly song over and over.

9. If you snap and get angry (which is okay when you are stressed) apologize to your victim. Let them know that you were stressed and took it out on them, and you didn't mean to. Mean it when you apologize.

10. Put on great music, then dance, tap your fingers and smile, remembering that without the bad times we can't appreciate the good times.

www.pegine.com
©2002, 2005, 2007 Pegine Echevarria

No. Life is not fair. It's a lesson, and lessons can get tricky. Sometimes the lesson is fun; sometimes it's not connected to any major emotions; sometimes it's pretty tough. The question is *what we learn* from any given situation.

When we train ourselves to look for the good that life gives us, we begin to appreciate the little things that aren't so little, the miraculous moments. I'm talking about moments like the applause from co-workers, the smell of a just-washed head of hair, or the feeling of triumph when we move past a fear. These moments help us appreciate life – whether it seems fair at the moment or not.

"When we look closely enough, we find our momentous 'AHA's!" hidden inside everyday moments"
~ **Pegine Echevarria, MSW~**

Try Its

Without (seemingly) unfair moments in your
past, you wouldn't be the unique, wise,
powerful person you have grown to be.

1. Write three of the biggest "No fair!"
    moments in your life. How did they
    feel at the time? What did you learn
    from them? How did your own actions
    helped or hinder your own personal
    growth?

2. Review how you described your
    lessons. Are they framed in a positive
    manner or do resentment or anger
    linger? If your perception of the lesson
    is still negative, change it.

3. If there is resentment, anger, or "poor
    me" language in any of your
    descriptions then *you are still blaming*
    and not learning. It is time to *learn and
    let go* of the blame, upset, and anger,
    because anger doesn't serve you and
    does nothing to the person you are

blaming or angry at. (Usually that person has no way of knowing how you are feeling.)

**Kick Butt
Actions**

Ask questions that challenge your beliefs
about situations that seemed "not fair" at the
time, and the roles you cast yourself in as a
result. For instance:

1. What is the opposite of a "martyr,"
   "victim" or "drama queen" reaction to
   this situation? Write your answers
   down.
2. When you are in the role of martyr,
   victim or drama queen and you choose
   to act the opposite way, what do you
   think will happen?
3. For me the opposite of
   - victim is *victor*,
   - martyr is *leader*,
   - drama queen is *power queen*.

What outcomes would *you* have in *your* life if
you accepted these opposite behaviors as your

reality for dealing with the *next* "not fair!"
situation you encounter?

Customer Service: All in the Family

As individuals, each of us has a business - the business of life. But what foot do we put forward with the "customers" in our own family? During crisis situations that can have a lifetime effect on our relationships, how do our actions affect those precious people? Do we analyze what we can do better next time, and truly strive to do it?

Let me describe a recent emergency within my family, and review how I applied a technique I often use in business customer service situations to my family situation.

When my mom had the operation, the crisis was immediate and unexpected. I heard about it as I was 1,000 miles from home, stranded in a crowded airport and facing long departure delays. I was distraught and upset. I felt disempowered, frustrated, and sad.

As time progressed, I became self-involved. My emotions and my concerns for my mom and dad were of major importance. At that crisis time, I was not focusing on my husband, my children or my brother. I'll admit it -- I wasn't exactly pleasant to be around. Didn't they understand my problem? Couldn't they read my mind and give me what I needed? Couldn't they help me maintain calmness in this time of turbulence?

These are the same thoughts that customer service representatives think in times of crisis. "I'm stressed! Don't you think I am trying to fix the problem? I'm doing all I can with the resources I have!" In the face of a crisis and high frustration, the customer service representative may even blame the problem or his/her behavior on others.

I found myself deep into this negative behavior. I forced myself to step back and self-analyze. This was not easy because it was simply easier to blame others. I asked myself:

- How am I choosing to behave during this crisis?

- Am I clearly communicating my problem to others?

- Which are actual problems, and which are simply minor challenges?

- Am I putting the whole situation in proper context in life's bigger picture?

- Is my behavior "productive or non-productive"? (This is a question my family frequently asks each other.)

- How can I clearly communicate solutions?

- Where can I get help?

When we are dealing with an irate customer, our focus is to maintain a calm demeanor, listen to the client, repeat the problem to ensure we understand their issue, and offer available solutions. Our goal is to keep this customer as a lifelong friend of our business.

So -- I decided to take those lessons in business customer service and apply them to family customer service. I asked myself the same questions I had trained customer service people to ask. We could all benefit from asking those kinds of questions now and then, couldn't we?

Are we maintaining personal tranquility so that we communicate calmness to others? Are we listening? Can we clearly articulate the problem? Are we moving from placing blame to focusing on the real issue? And, do we need to offer a solution, or just listen?

The family is where the long-term relationship is truly defined. We really are responsible for our behavior there. We need to know when to offer solutions, when to ask for help, and when to look elsewhere for assistance.

What would happen if we thought of each crisis as an opportunity to *strengthen* our relationships within our family?

Quote

"Keep your fork. The best is yet to come"

~Pegine Echevarria, MSW~

Try Its

Recently I received a story about a woman who was dying.

She spoke to her rabbi about her funeral arrangements. She asked to be buried with a fork in her hand. "Why?" the rabbi asked.

"When I was a child I learned how important a fork is to one's life. Every time I went to a restaurant or some important occasion the host or waiter would say, 'Keep your fork.' I quickly learned that that always meant that something wonderful and delicious was coming, a piece of scrumptious chocolate cake or something deliciously sweet and drippy and gooey."

www.pegine.com
©2002, 2005, 2007 Pegine Echevarria

"As I aged," she continued, "I learned that life was exactly the same. If I 'kept my fork,' that meant I could choose to anticipate that all the good things would continue coming would come my way, and would get better. They always did, one way or another."

"Now that I'm dying, I'm anticipating a great afterlife, so I want to keep my fork."

Her faith in the process of optimism always brought her the good fortune of long-term perspective in her family relationships … and in all her relationships. Her attitude created the outcomes she wanted throughout her life – and, for all I know, in the afterlife as well. Yours can, too.

Kick Butt
Actions

For the last sixty days I've been writing the
following prayer once a day, a line at a time,
and then writing my own perceptions and
feelings about that line. The gifts I've been
receiving after doing so have been (there is no
other word) miraculous.

Read it. It's the Jabez prayer from the Old
Testament.

Bless me indeed,
Expand my territory,
That your hand would be in mine.
Keep me from evil,
That I cause no pain. (1 Chronicles, 4-10)

Each day I write about the prayer I have
written down. Writing about that prayer has
given me hope in uncertain times, and
brought extraordinary resources my way.

Writing about that prayer unleashed an excitement about my life and my relationships, the kind of excitement that a child feels before a major holiday. Writing about that prayer made me aware of my frailties and the need for help. Writing about that prayer also made me acknowledge the negative attitudes, thoughts, and worries that make me lash out at others unnecessarily.

My life moved to another level by incorporating this prayer into my life. Try it and see what happens in your life!

Epilogue: Discipline Equals Results

Productive routines, tested processes, organized desks -- yuck!

I always feel like I've been sent back to high school when I try to approach these subjects. Why do we rebel against the things that in reality would make our lives easier and better?

As young children we heard our parents talking about *discipline*. We began to associate discipline with *punishment*. Yet they are two completely different things.

According to Merriam-Webster's Collegiate Dictionary, punishment is defined as "suffering, pain, or loss that serves as retribution; a penalty inflicted on an offender through judicial procedure or severe, rough, or disastrous treatment". On the other hand, discipline is defined as "training that corrects molds, or perfects the mental faculties or moral character; control gained by enforcing obedience or order; orderly or prescribed conduct or pattern of behavior".

Think of discipline as a *measuring tool* that actually helps you produce results ... when used in moderation. Sometimes we can be a little too disciplined and go overboard. We all know people who are over disciplined but not necessarily well rounded. They may be disciplined in cleaning their homes, making all of their calls, or doing the same thing day in and day out – no matter what. They may be less disciplined in the softer areas, such as contacting and reaching out to others, opening themselves to spontaneity, and being sensitive to those around them.

The character played by Robert De Niro in the movie *Meet the Parents* is an example of such a person. He is hyper-disciplined, to the point that he is oblivious to the human need for contact and communication in his own family.

He is so obsessive in his ways that he overlooks his daughter's feelings and is unable to see how his behavior is causing others to behave irrationally. While it is true that life without discipline is a mess, too much discipline can sometimes seem to extinguish our very humanity.

Discipline in moderation and with clarity, however, moves our lives forward. When we become disciplined in bill paying, our credit goes up. When we are disciplined about making our beds in the morning and cleaning up after ourselves, we feel better about our homes. When we are disciplined about our eating and exercise habits, then we are trimmer and healthier.

In business, discipline plays a major role in our success. Setting up a marketing plan and sales plan for our businesses is the first step. It is our discipline that motivates us, on a daily basis, to implement the plan and make a difference in how our businesses grow.

Often, there will be days when we simply don't feel like doing something we associate with discipline: exercising, making cold calls, sending out the letters we promised. When we don't do the tasks we promised ourselves that we would do, we are likely to begin the process of negative thinking. We tell ourselves "See, there's the proof -- you aren't as good as you thought." This kind of negative thinking leads us to even more unproductive negative thinking, which further erodes our confidence. It's a bad cycle.

As I close this book, I want to leave you with some strategies you can use to help yourself become more *constructively* disciplined in all areas of your life. Here are five ideas.

1. *Have a plan for the day.* Don't make it a long list. Start by limiting it to three things. Focus on your work. What item absolutely must get accomplished? That's number one. Then you might write down what food you will eat and when you will exercise. That's number

two. What's number three? Keep it
very simple at first.

2. *As you do each task,* check the item off
   the list. As in physically writing the
   check mark on the piece of paper.
   There is a terrific feeling that comes
   with formally acknowledging to
   yourself that you have in fact
   accomplished a task on your to-do list.
   Try it!

3. *Call someone with whom you can share
   your plan.* In the beginning it may
   require two calls a day. For the last
   five years I have had a 'buddy' who I
   can always call to stay on task. You
   should, too.

4. *Create a routine -- and start small.* Yes,
   you do to know what I mean. Make
   the small, simple choices that reduce
   stress in your day. Put your keys in the
   same place. Make your sales and
   customer calls at the same time each
   day. Write your memos at the same

time. In this way, you stop "churning" about when something will get done -- because you have already established the time in your day when that thing takes place, or the way a given process works.

5. *Acknowledge yourself in a positive way when you complete all the items on your list.* Write yourself a note saying great job -- or just take a moment to note the satisfying feeling you get from being disciplined.

Discipline is actually the positive feeling you get from identifying the process that delivers results you like. Discipline is a freeing experience, a strategy for relaxation, and a great tool for building your own self-esteem. Discipline is the difference between dreaming and achieving your dream – calmly but purposefully. Start today and take the (easy) first steps to becoming constructively disciplined.

Notes

About the Author

Former girl gang member from the Bronx, Pegine Echevarria, is a member of a new "gang" that even her feisty single mom would approve. Pegine's fellow "gang members" include such luminaries as Dale Carnegie, Zig Zigler and Tony Robbins. They are all members of the Motivational Speakers Hall of Fame, and Pegine is its first Latina inductee.

From teen gang member and receptionist to VP of sales and business owner, Pegine moved rapidly up the ladder of the corporate and non-profit world. However, when her professional speaking business collapsed after 9/11, Pegine morphed into a stand-up comedian to motivate people and pay the bills.

Pegine's can-do attitude is the product of her mom's strength and her determination to survive the streets, and is reflected in her aptly titled book, *Sometimes You Have To Kick Your Own Butt*. Pegine's unique background, and her bold, comedic style, makes her message of empowerment accessible to a more diverse audience. She is an expert on motivating leaders in a diverse world and empowering people to be leaders in their lives, work, family, and community.

www.pegine.com

Called the empress of empowerment and guru in leading in a diverse world, Pegine's clientele includes Verizon, Merrill Lynch, New York Life Insurance, the U.S. Military, and others. Her current national positions include the *Society of Human Resources National Workplace Diversity Expertise Panel*, Advisory board of the *Jacksonville Women's Business Center*, and *National Speakers Association* (minority outreach committee). Pegine is also a national board member and Vice President, of *Employers United for a Stronger America* – a foundation which provides research, about employers and their US military reserve and US National Guard employees as well as fundraising for programs that serve them.

Pegine, who has a Masters in Social Work in Group and Organizational Development, has focused her wide array of talents into inspiring thousands of lives. A recipient of numerous awards and proclamations for her leadership, Pegine is a 2007 nominee for Hispanic Business Magazine's Woman of the Year. She is also the 2005 MED Week Entrepreneur of the Year in North Florida.

Not too shabby for a former gang member from the Bronx.

www.pegine.com
©2002, 2005, 2007 Pegine Echevarria

Books by Pegine:

Sometimes You Need To Kick Your Own Butt
For All Our Daughters: How Mentoring Helps Young
Women and Girls Master the Art of Growing Up
Breaking Through: Getting Past the Stuck Points in
Your Life (edited by Barbara Stanny (Contributing
Author)
Go Fish for Friends, Business, and Opportunities

Soon look for:
Bragging Rights - Transform Your Team in 21 Days
White Men are Diverse Too!
Communicating Your V.A.L.U.E.
Play BIG Reach Your Potential
Transformational Recruiters - Working with Civilians

Go to

www.pegine.com

or call

(904) 280-8806